Dress-up Day

written by Jay Dale
illustrated by Heather Heyworth

"Good morning, Tom,"
said Miss Flora.
"Why are you dressed up today?"

"It's Dress-up Day," said Tom.

"Oh, no!" said Miss Flora.
"I forgot it was Dress-up Day!"

All the children started to come in.

Bec was a tiny fairy.
Amber was a big yellow banana.
And Lee was a fluffy cat.
All the children were dressed up.

Bec and Tom were looking sad.
Meg looked sad, too.

"Miss Flora," said Bec.
"You did not dress up today."

"All the teachers are dressed up," said Tom.

Miss Flora smiled at the children.
"Come with me," she said.
"I will dress up today!"

Miss Flora took the children to a big room.

"Look!" said Miss Flora.
"Here is a dress-up box.
Let's look inside."

Tom opened the box.
He took out a yellow wig.
He put it on Miss Flora's head.

Bec took out a red ball with a string.
She put it on Miss Flora's nose.

"You look funny!" laughed Meg.
"You look like a funny clown."

"Yes!" said Miss Flora.
"I will dress up like a clown.
You can all help me."

"Here are some big pink trousers," said Bec.

"And here is a big blue shirt," smiled Lee.

"Look!" said Tom.

"Here are some funny red shoes."

Miss Flora looked like a funny clown.
She did a silly little dance.

"You look funny,"
laughed all the children.

"Yes," smiled Miss Flora.
"Dress-up Day is lots of fun!"